21 encouraging BIBLE VERSES
to help beat the winter blues!

written & designed by Shalana Frisby

First Printing: November 2018
1 2 3 Journal It Publishing

ISBN-13: 978-1-947209-93-0

 Table of Contents

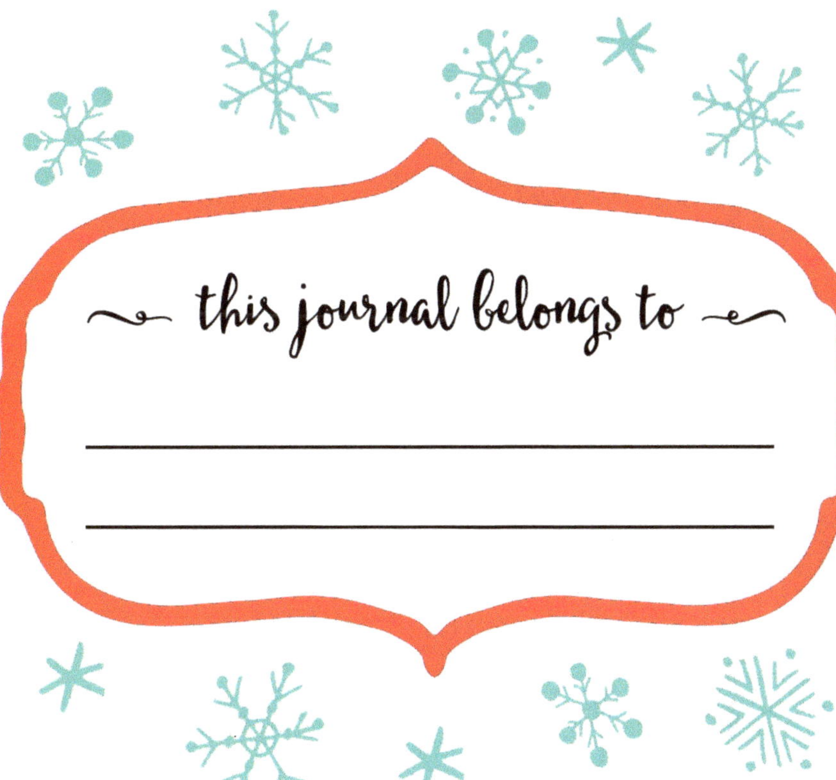
this journal belongs to

But they that wait
upon the Lord shall renew
their strength; they shall
mount up with wings as
eagles; they shall run, and
not be weary; and they
shall walk, and not faint.

ISAIAH 40:31

Prayer Requests & Praise for Answers　　　　　Gratitude for People & Things

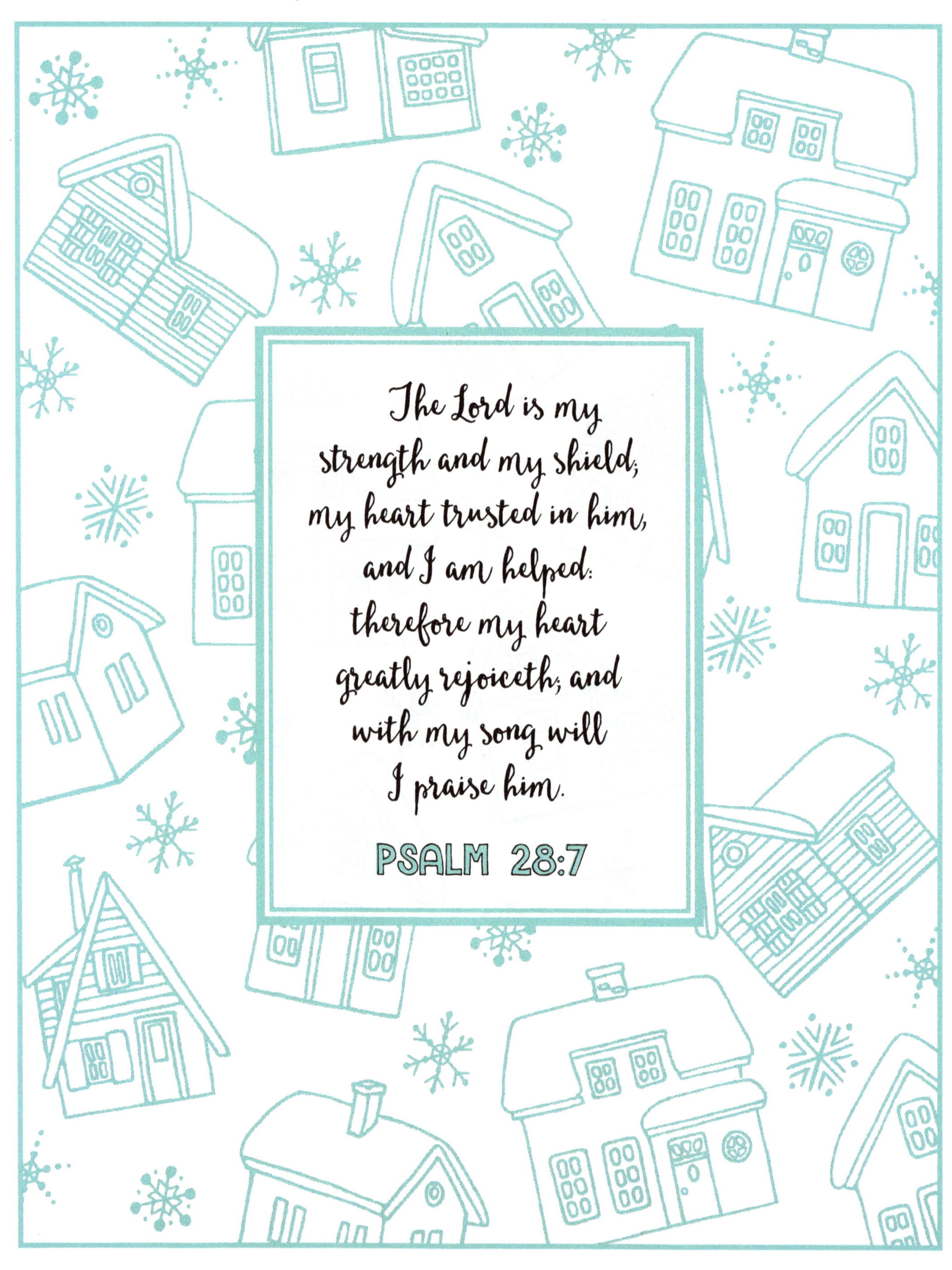

The Lord is my
strength and my shield;
my heart trusted in him,
and I am helped:
therefore my heart
greatly rejoiceth; and
with my song will
I praise him.

PSALM 28:7

~ Study Notes ~

Prayer Requests & Praise for Answers

Gratitude for People & Things

And we know that
all things work together
for good to them that
love God, to them who
are the called according
to his purpose.

ROMANS 8:28

Study Notes

Prayer Requests & Praise for Answers

Gratitude for People & Things

Blessed is the man that
endureth temptation: for
when he is tried, he shall
receive the crown of life,
which the Lord hath
promised to them
that love him.
JAMES 1:12

Prayer Requests & Praise for Answers

Gratitude for People & Things

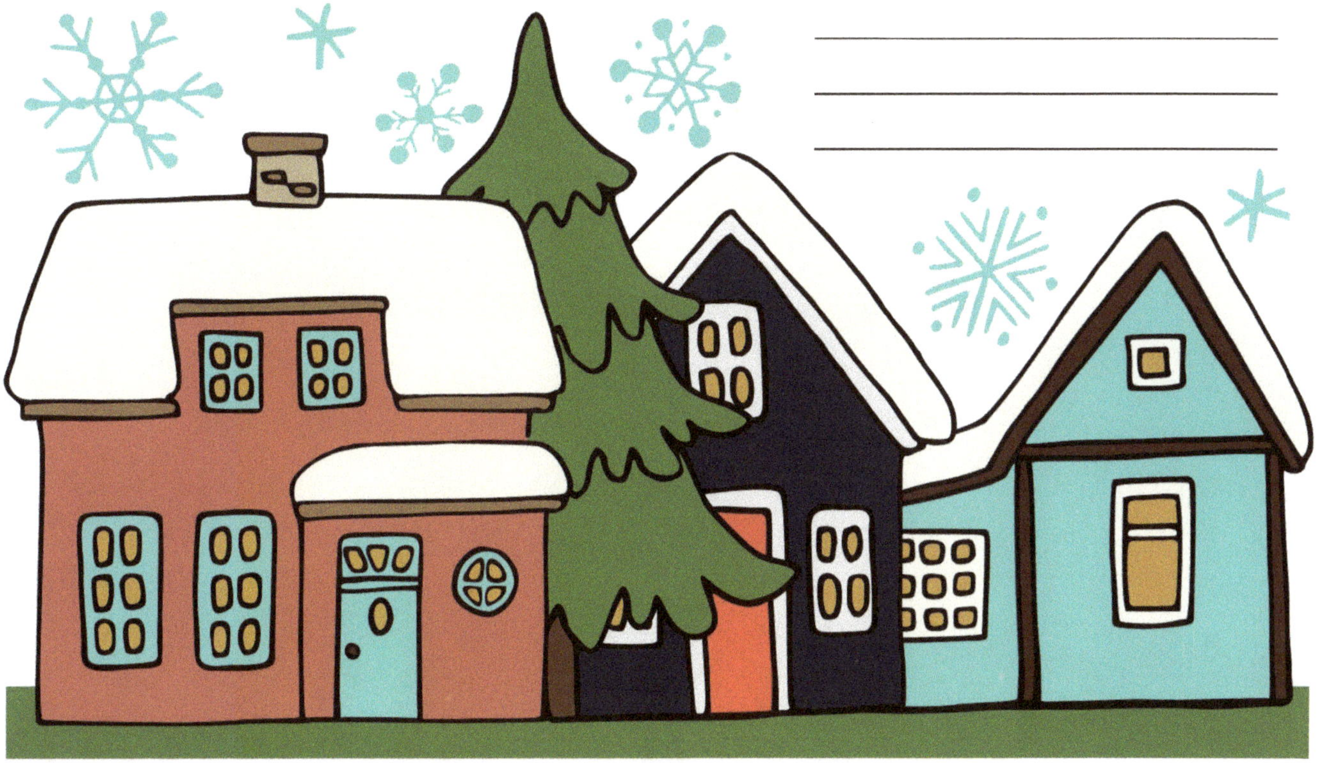

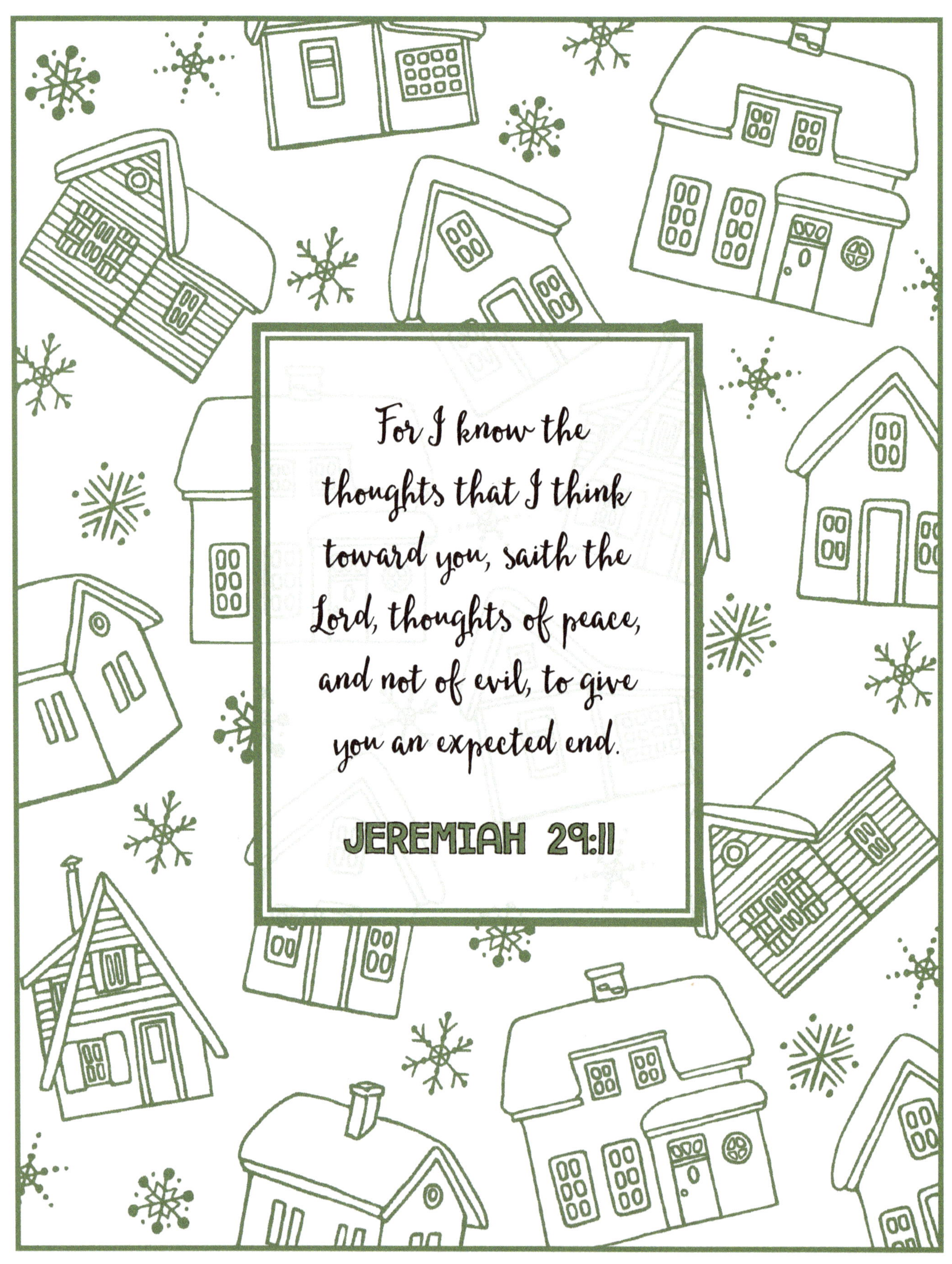

For I know the
thoughts that I think
toward you, saith the
Lord, thoughts of peace,
and not of evil, to give
you an expected end.

JEREMIAH 29:11

Study Notes

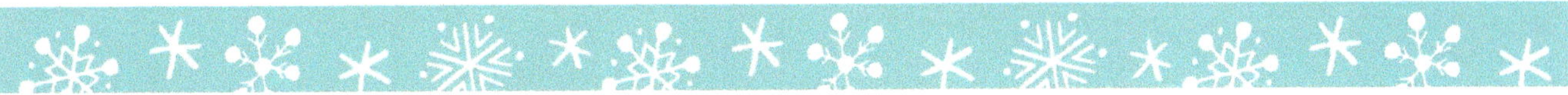

Prayer Requests & Praise for Answers

Gratitude for People & Things

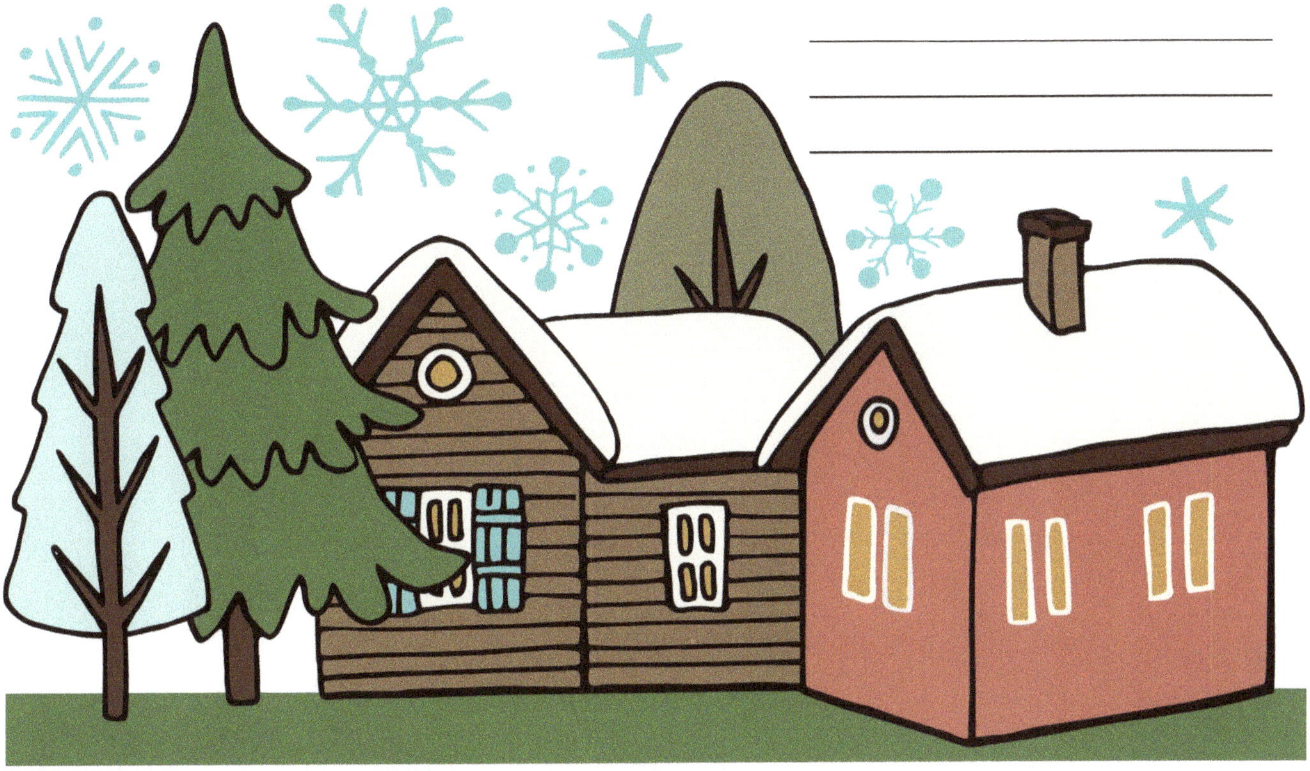

And let us not be
weary in well doing: for
in due season we shall
reap, if we faint not.

GALATIANS 6:9

Study Notes

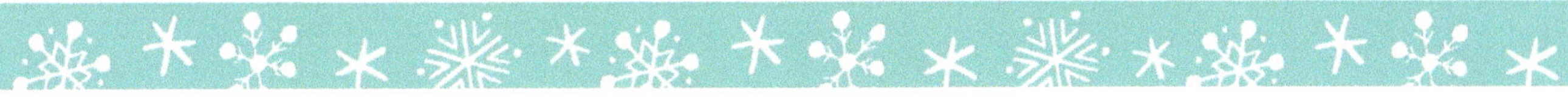

Prayer Requests & Praise for Answers

Gratitude for People & Things

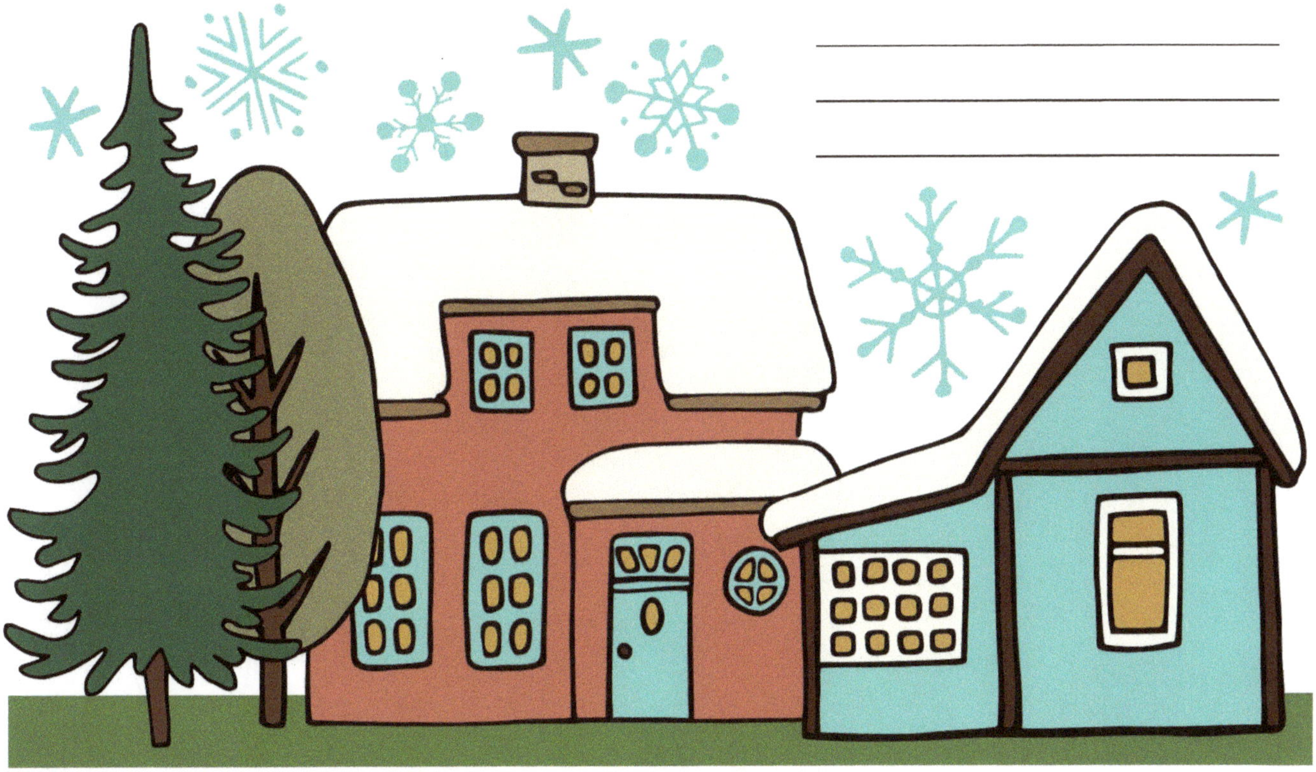

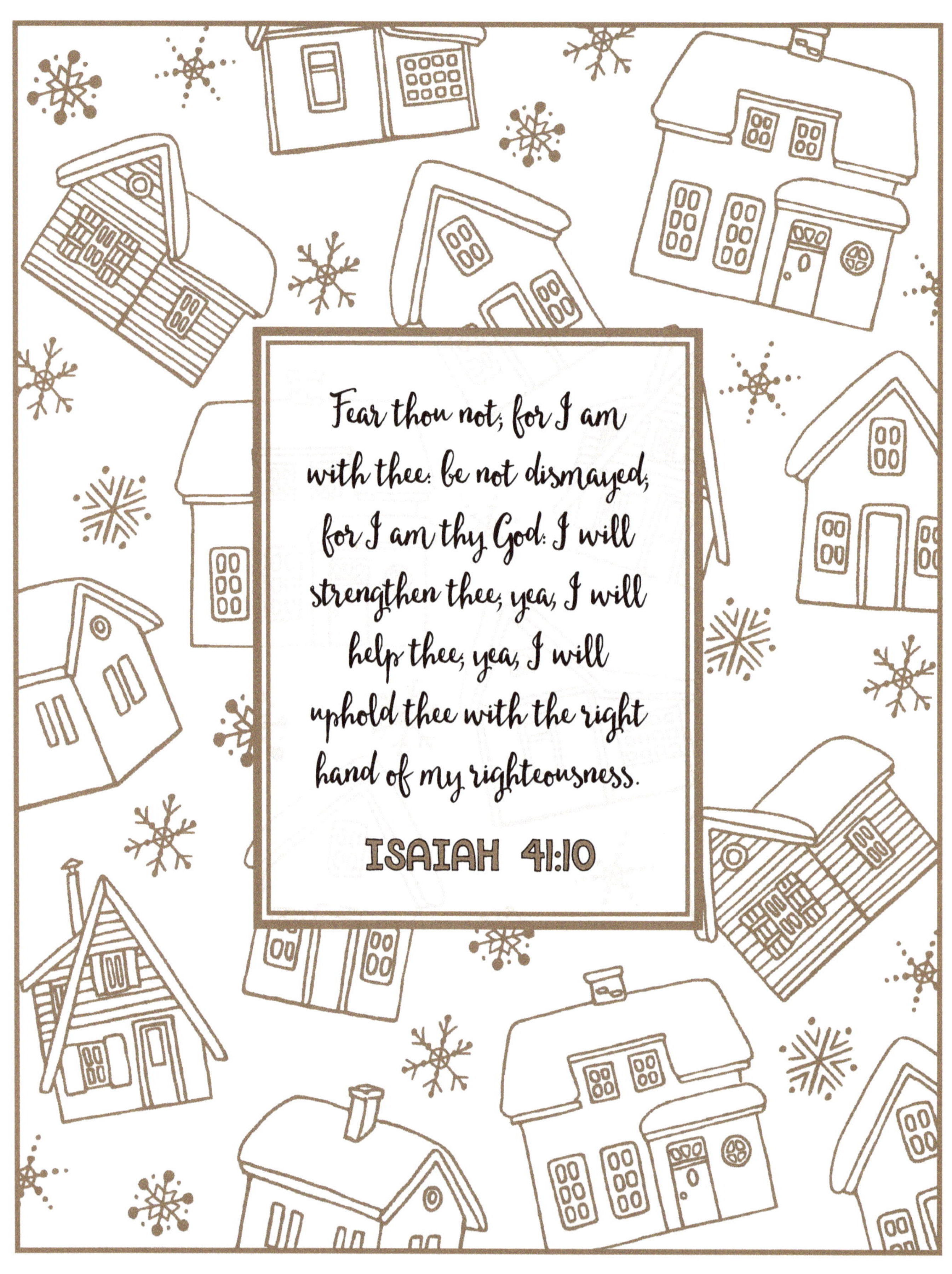

Fear thou not; for I am with thee: be not dismayed; for I am thy God: I will strengthen thee; yea, I will help thee; yea, I will uphold thee with the right hand of my righteousness.

ISAIAH 41:10

Prayer Requests & Praise for Answers

Gratitude for People & Things

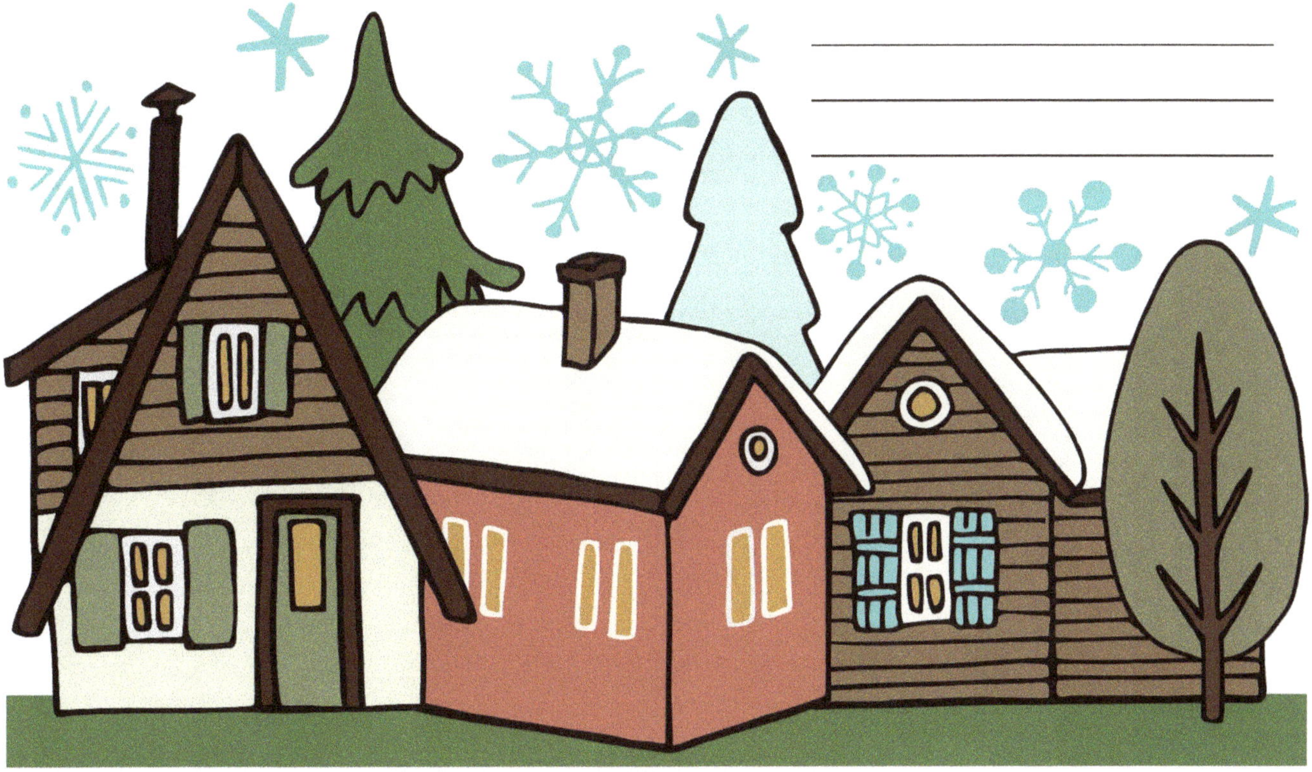

Beloved, I wish above all things that thou mayest prosper and be in health, even as thy soul prospereth.

3 JOHN 2

~ Study Notes ~

Prayer Requests & Praise for Answers

Gratitude for People & Things

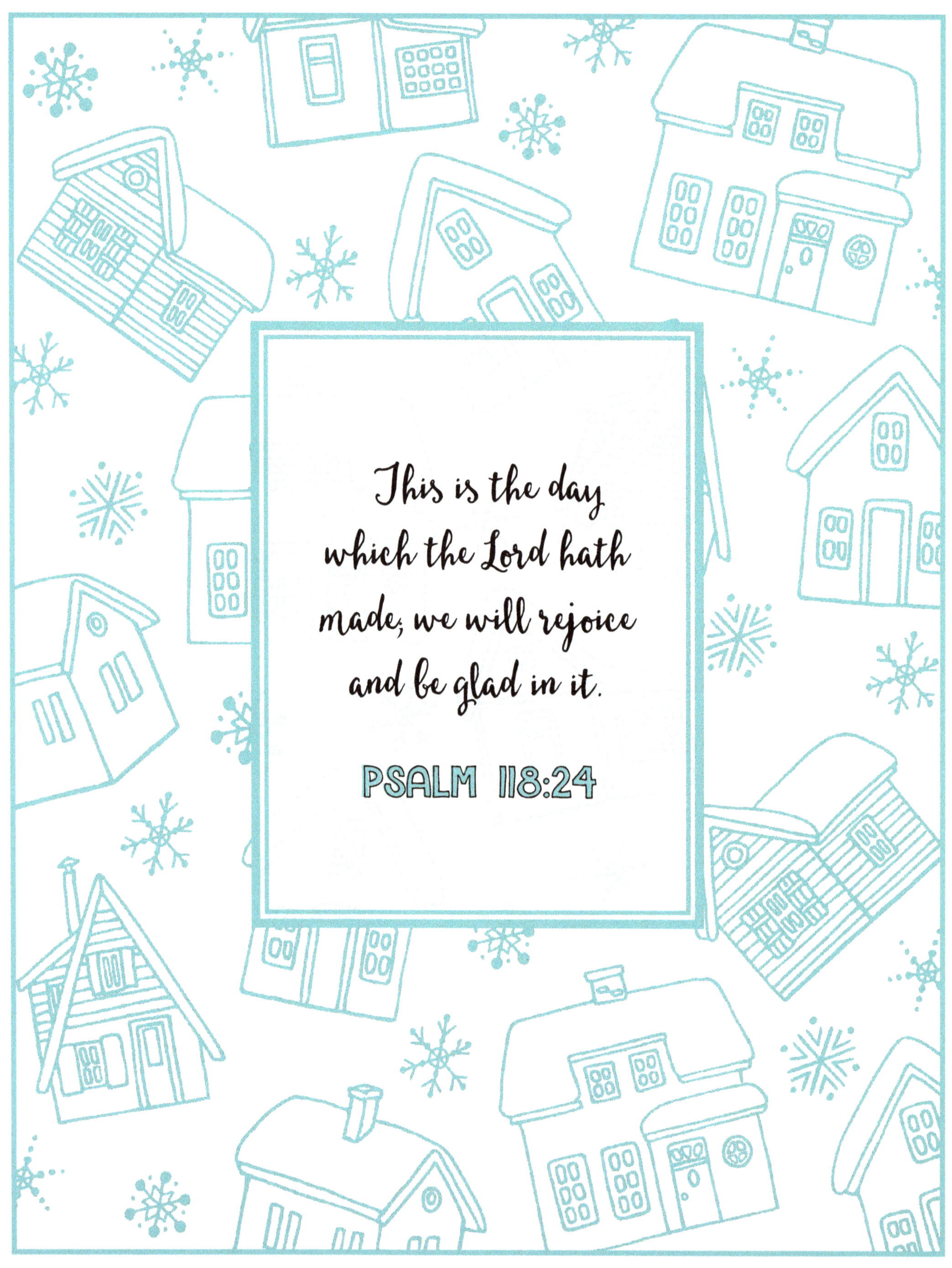
This is the day
which the Lord hath
made; we will rejoice
and be glad in it.

PSALM 118:24

Prayer Requests & Praise for Answers

Gratitude for People & Things

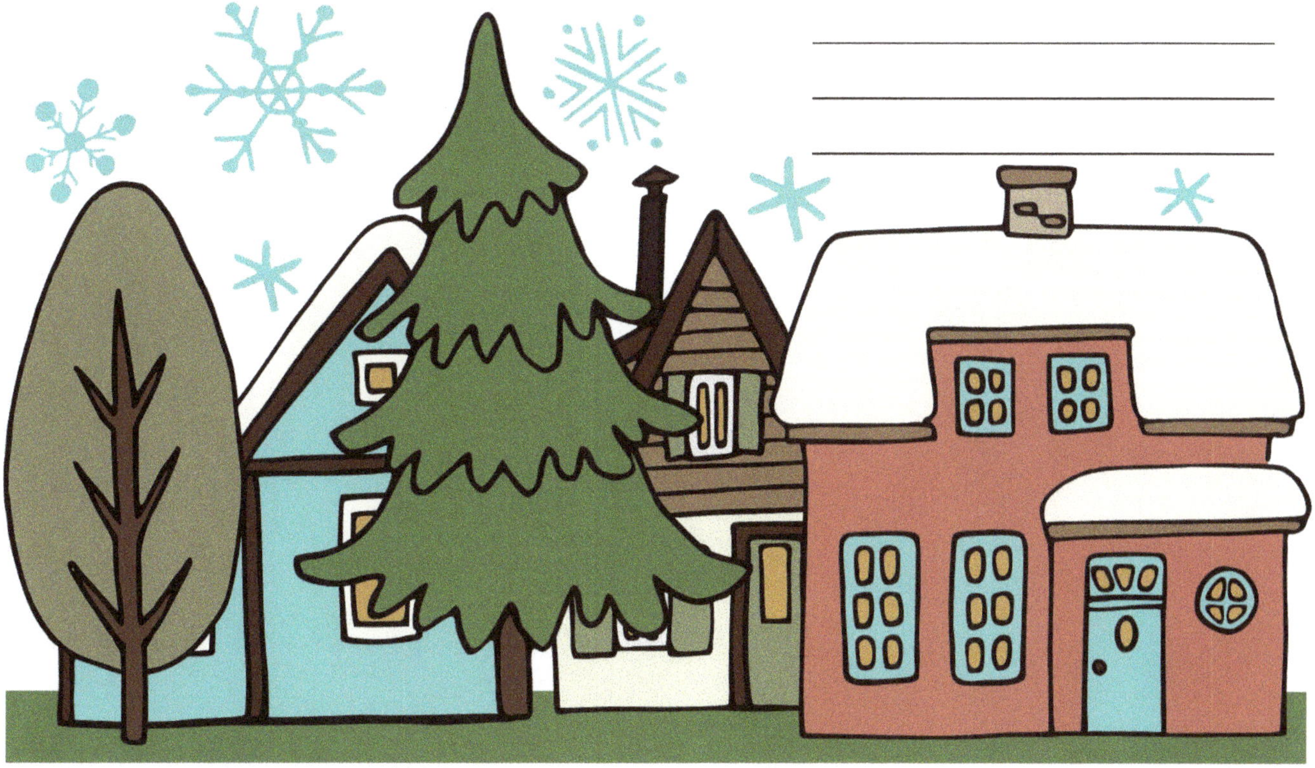

Every man according
as he purposeth in his
heart, so let him give;
not grudgingly, or of
necessity: for God loveth
a cheerful giver.

2 CORINTHIANS 9:7

Prayer Requests & Praise for Answers

Gratitude for People & Things

I can do all things
through Christ which
strengtheneth me.

PHILIPPIANS 4:13

Prayer Requests & Praise for Answers

Gratitude for People & Things

Delight thyself also
in the Lord: and he shall
give thee the desires of
thine heart.

PSALM 37:4

Prayer Requests & Praise for Answers

Gratitude for People & Things

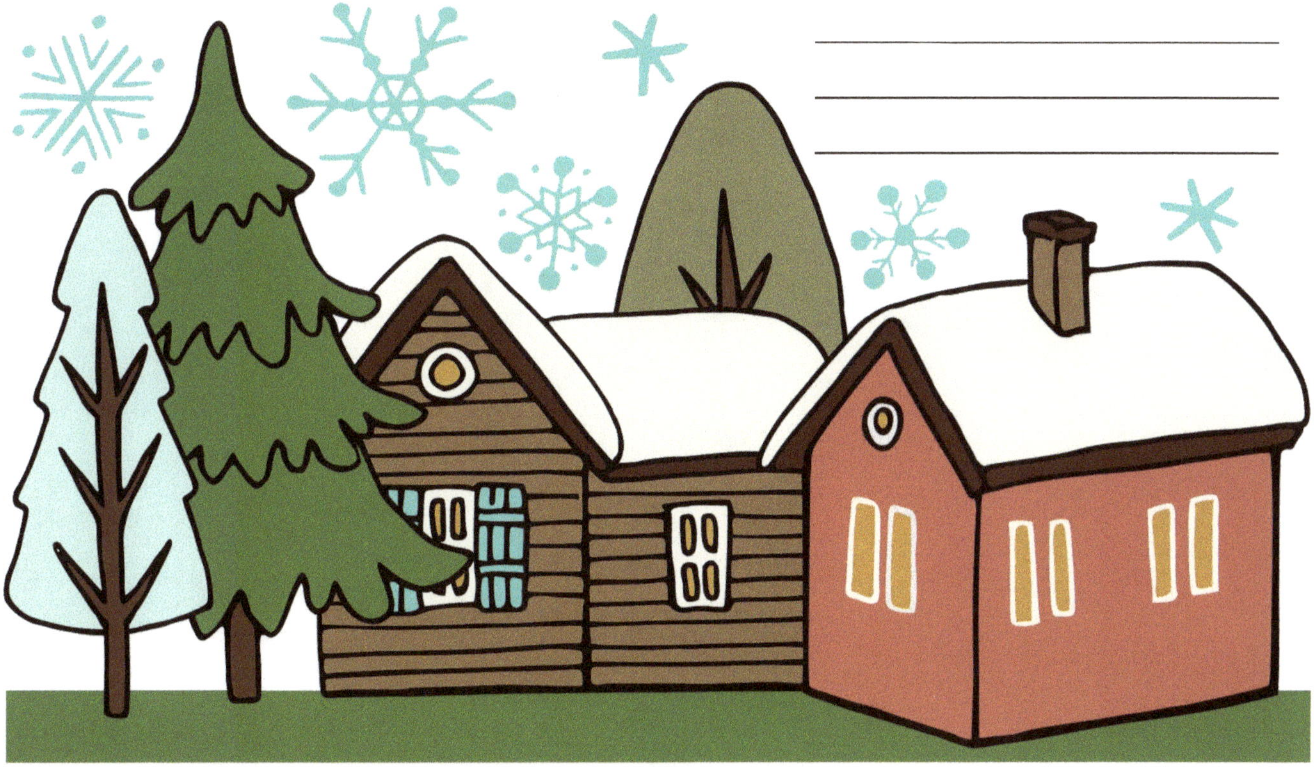

Be strong and of a
good courage, fear not,
nor be afraid of them:
for the Lord thy God, he
it is that doth go with
thee; he will not fail
thee, nor forsake thee.

DEUTERONOMY 31:6

Prayer Requests & Praise for Answers

Gratitude for People & Things

The name of the
Lord is a strong tower:
the righteous runneth
into it, and is safe.

PROVERBS 18:10

Prayer Requests & Praise for Answers

Gratitude for People & Things

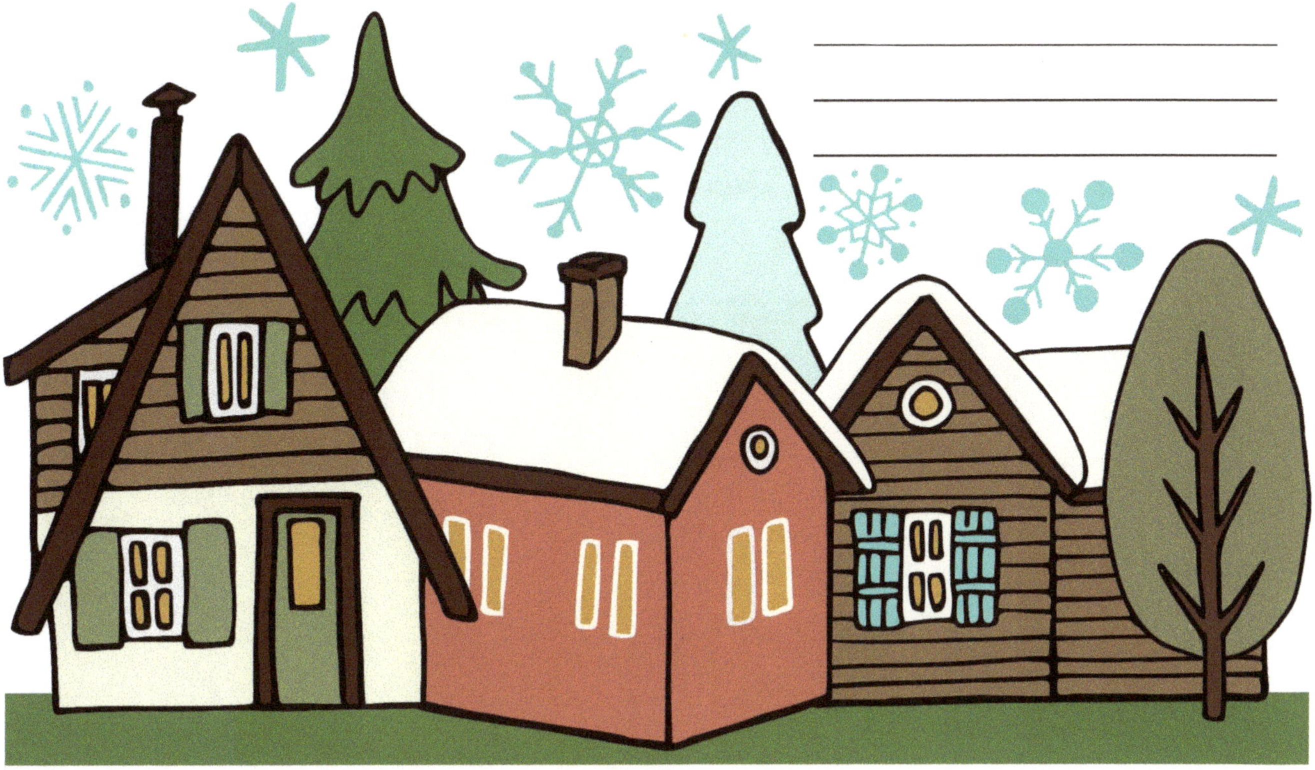

Now the God of hope
fill you with all joy
and peace in believing,
that ye may abound in
hope, through the power
of the Holy Ghost.

ROMANS 15:13

Prayer Requests & Praise for Answers

Gratitude for People & Things

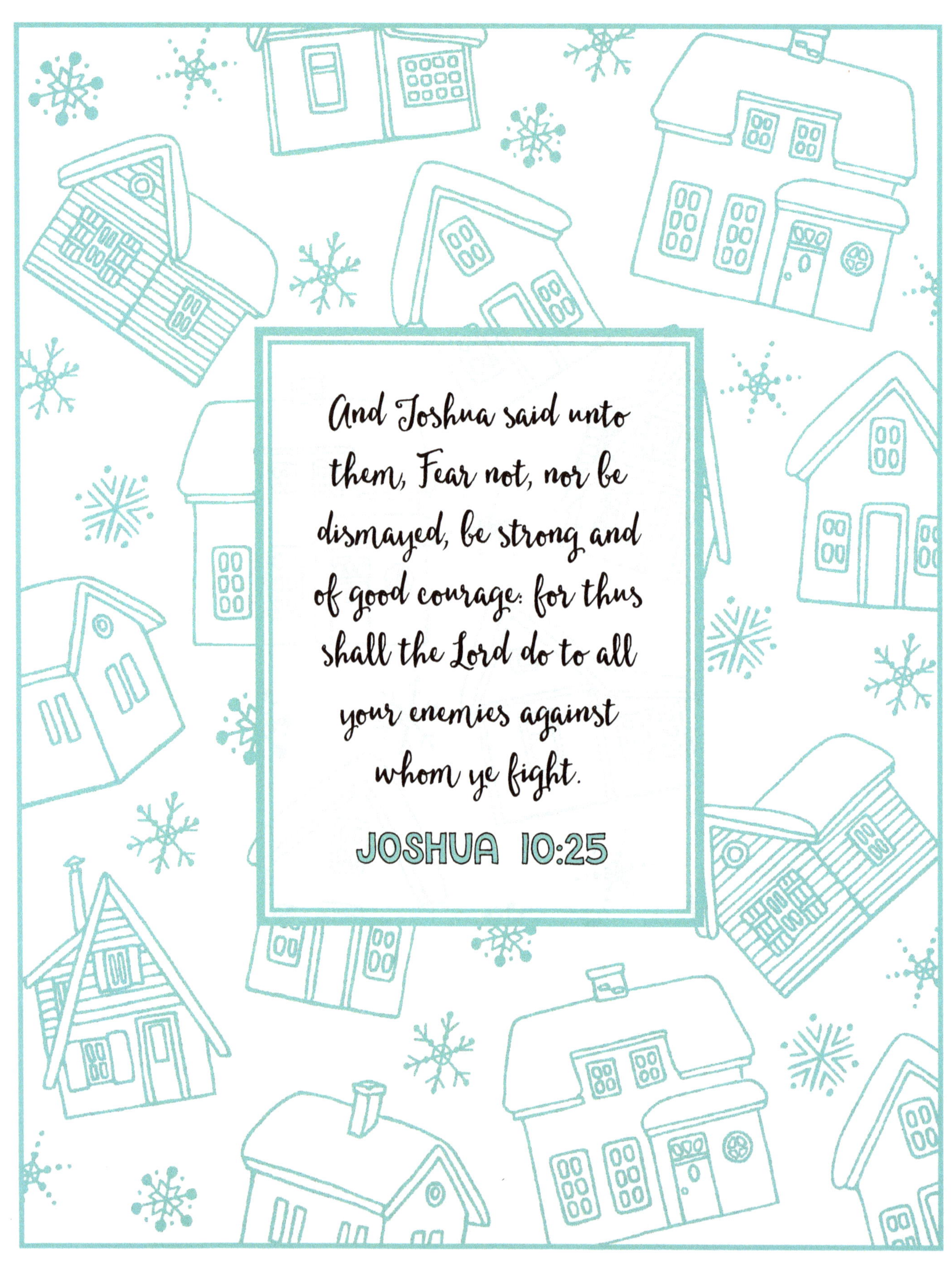

And Joshua said unto them, Fear not, nor be dismayed, be strong and of good courage: for thus shall the Lord do to all your enemies against whom ye fight.

JOSHUA 10:25

Prayer Requests & Praise for Answers

Gratitude for People & Things

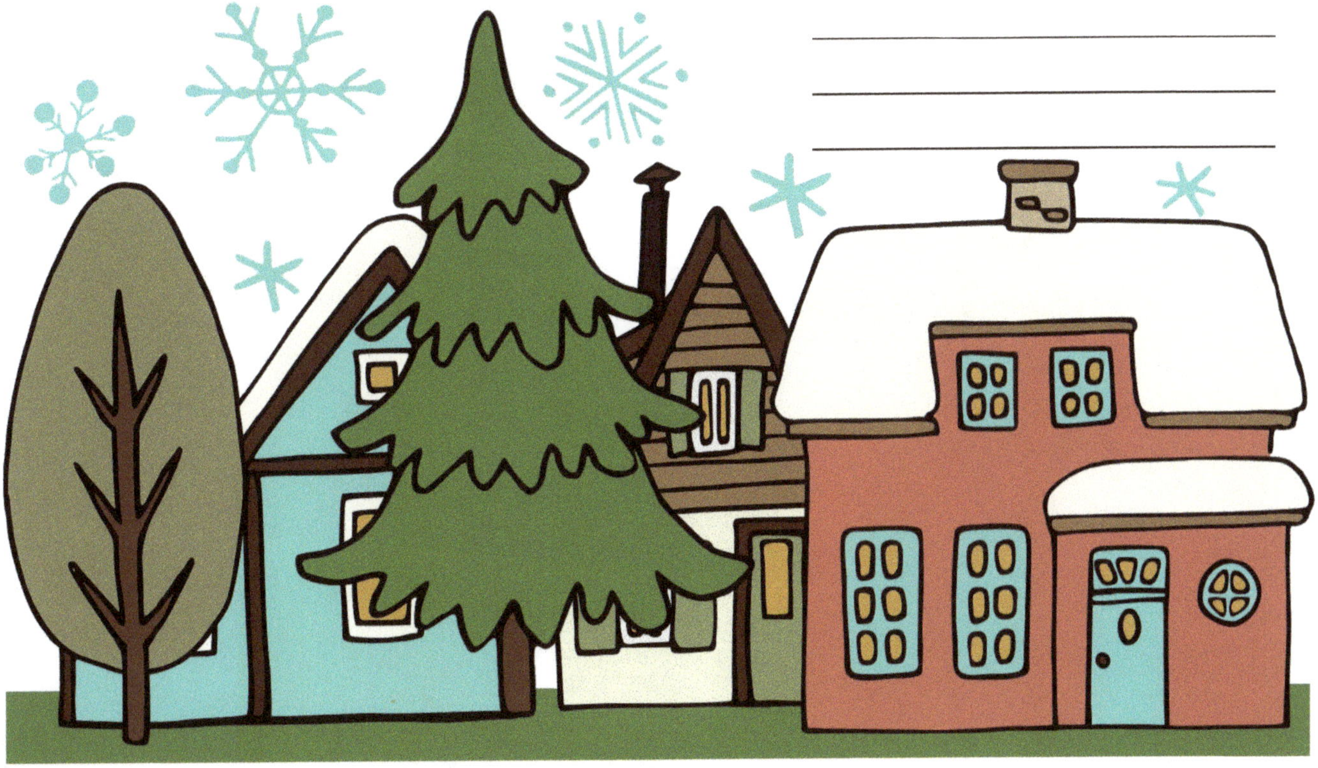

God is not a man, that he should lie; neither the son of man, that he should repent: hath he said, and shall he not do it? or hath he spoken, and shall he not make it good?
NUMBERS 23:19

____
____
____
____
____
____

Prayer Requests & Praise for Answers

Gratitude for People & Things

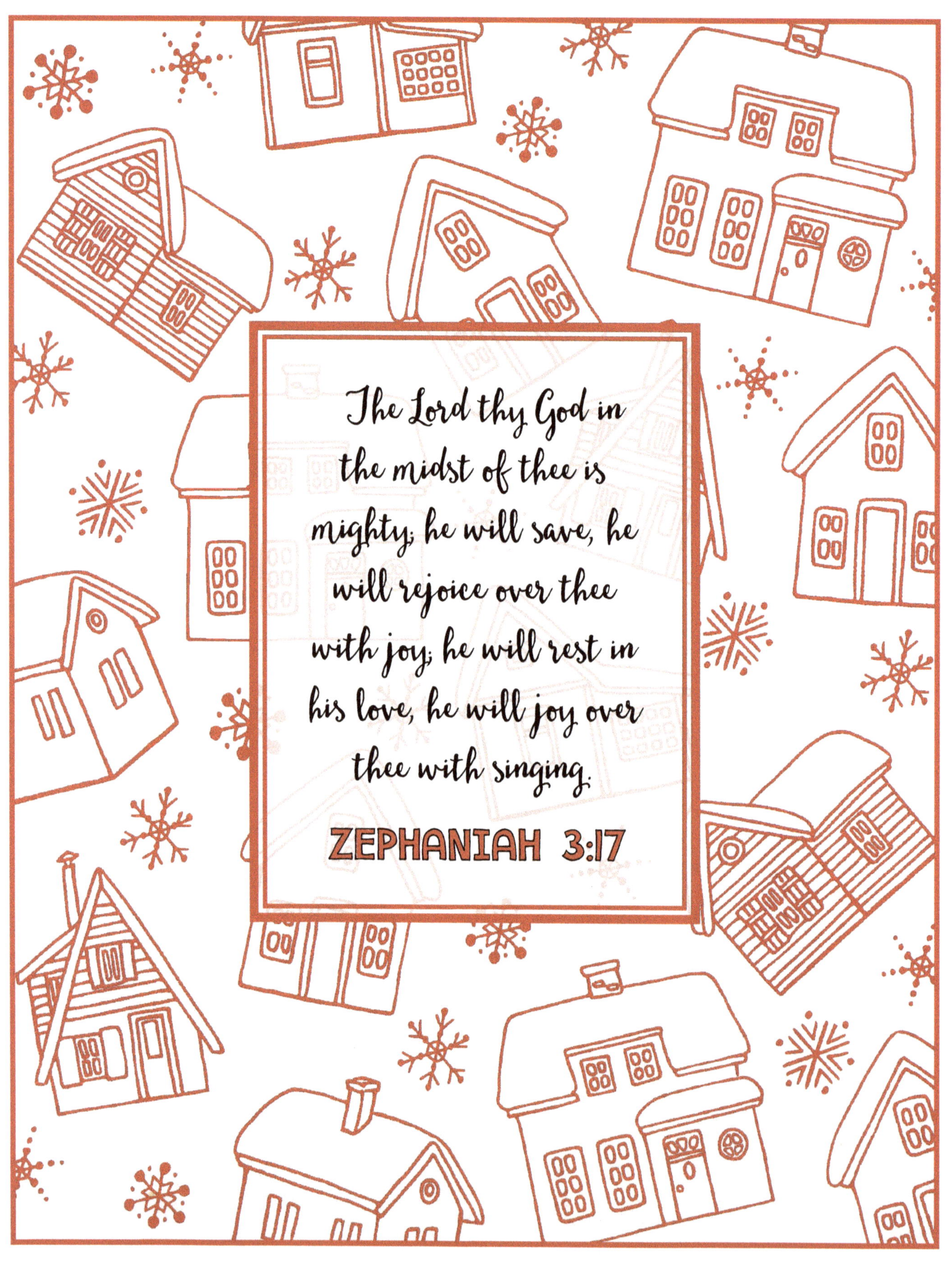

The Lord thy God in the midst of thee is mighty; he will save, he will rejoice over thee with joy; he will rest in his love, he will joy over thee with singing.
ZEPHANIAH 3:17

Prayer Requests & Praise for Answers

Gratitude for People & Things

Finally, brethren, whatsoever
things are true, whatsoever things
are honest, whatsoever things are
just, whatsoever things are pure,
whatsoever things are lovely,
whatsoever things are of good
report; if there be any virtue,
and if there be any praise,
think on these things.

PHILIPPIANS 4:8

Prayer Requests & Praise for Answers

Gratitude for People & Things

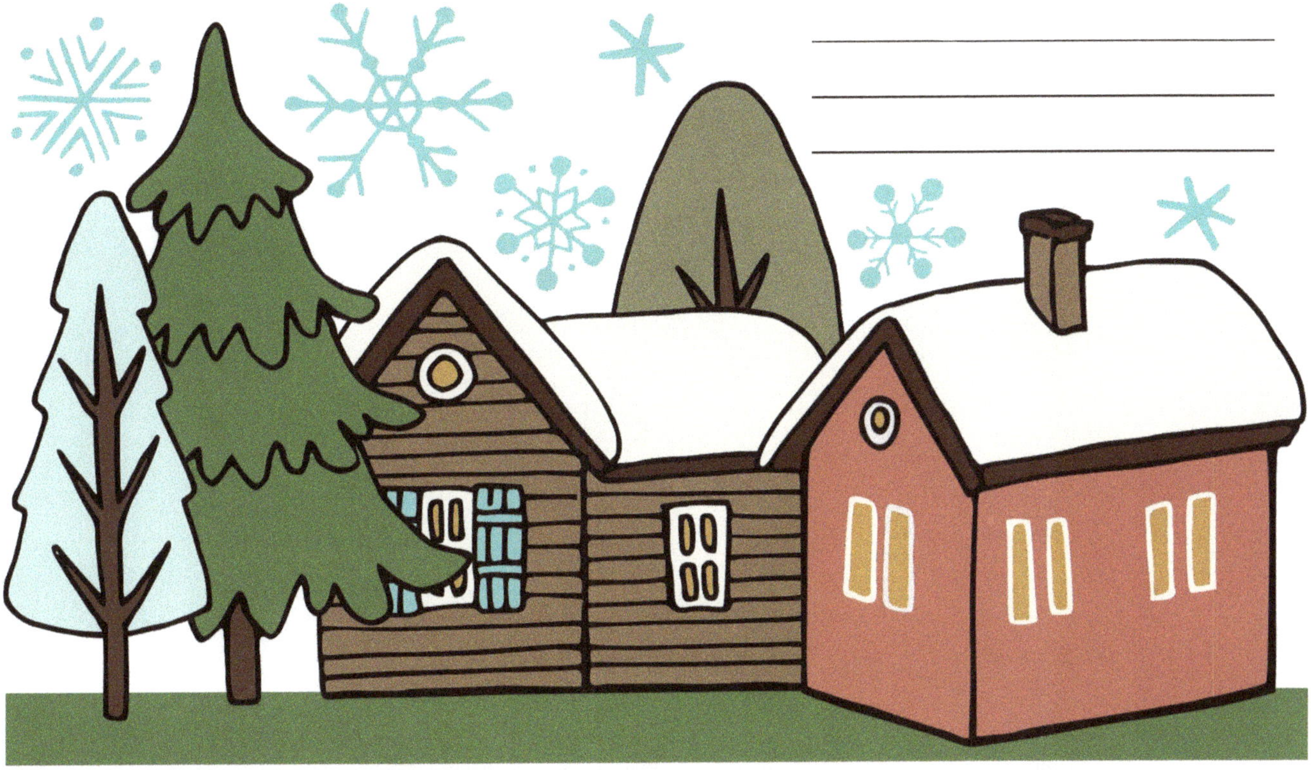

Now faith is the substance of things hoped for, the evidence of things not seen.

HEBREWS 11:1

Prayer Requests & Praise for Answers

Gratitude for People & Things

For God so loved the world, that he gave his only begotten Son, that whosoever believeth in him should not perish, but have everlasting life.
JOHN 3:16

Prayer Requests & Praise for Answers

Gratitude for People & Things

Extra Notes